DISPLAY

ONLY

FOR DISPLAY PURPOSES ONLY

DAVID SEYMOUR

Coach House Books
Toronto

first edition

 Canada Council   Conseil des Arts    ONTARIO ARTS COUNCIL   Canadä
for the Arts   du Canada   CONSEIL DES ARTS DE L'ONTARIO

Published with the generous assistance of the Canada Council for the Arts and
the Ontario Arts Council. Coach House Books also acknowledges the support
of the Government of Canada through the Canada Book Fund and the Govern-
ment of Ontario through the Ontario Book Publishing Tax Credit.

LIBRARY AND ARCHIVES CANADA CATALOGUING IN PUBLICATION

Seymour, David, 1971-
      For display purposes only / David Seymour.

Poems.
Issued also in electronic format.
ISBN 978-1-55245-274-5

      I. Title.

PS8637.E95F67 2013   C811'.6   C2013-900222-7

For Display Purposes Only is available as an ebook: ISBN 978 1 77056 341 4.

Purchase of the print version of this book entitles you to a free digital copy. To
claim your ebook of this title, please email sales@chbooks.com with proof of
purchase or visit chbooks.com/digital. (Coach House Books reserves the right to
terminate the free digital download offer at any time.)

for Karen

Table of Contents

'You climb a mountain
leading seven men who look like you. They depend
on you for their safety. You climb higher
and higher until you are alone under a sun
gone pale in altitude. You climb above birds
and clouds. You are home in this atmosphere.'

– Richard Hugo

'From being to being an idea, nothing comes through that intact.'

– Jay Hopler

Wild Lines

The best design survives
a narrative compulsion

Adhere to your personality and I
guarantee prediction

As you radiate I'll collect you
analyze your information

When I tell you I love you
you smile like

Our old television advertising
a clearer HD television

There goes the apartment performing
accurate impersonations again

Our snuggly companion repetition
returns with a difference

Far more pleasurable
than pity or reprieve

Time is the classic dimension
and chronic plot point

We've hurt one another
and haven't been sorry

I love you in the radiant sense
of you emitting duration

The best design dissolves
into behaviour

Our rooms, our bed, our windows
and unused corners

Bungled angles, disturbed dust
bunnies and flakes of us

Eyewitness Testimony

The man who was killed died. The gun
had gone ballistic in the parking lot. Up 'til then
all he'd done was have nothing to lose.
His hair was growing right out of his face.

Earlier, from the precipitate sky, hail the size
of golf balls pelted the clubhouse. Errant
hail-sized golf balls shanked the clubhouse
before the golfers ran for cover from the weather.

This occurred. On the fringe of suburbs
and their evident neighbouring. The cars
remained parked in the lot where he fell,
immobile necessary machinery.

The woman at the scene sporting leopard-print
spandex was way too realistic. She lacked
conspicuous panty lines. Her description,
though relevant, was weapon focused.

The report from the shots fired was heard variably
as a calendar sliding off a kitchen wall and the after-
vacuum of implosion. With decibel fluctuation,
distance and Doppler effect, reports varied.

Between the houses backing onto the tenth green,
aphids gathered all sounds within the 250-
to 45,000-cycle range of their tympana
and slept uninterviewed in the shade of hydrangea.

The passing cab driver had the largest
hippocampus among the onlookers, being
the least lost. This was scientifically proven
though need not be mentioned in the final.

Others were directionless – what they saw
they now knew had never not happened –
wondering how they had arrived here,
how here arrives. Post-storm light

struck the police cruiser windshield,
behaving as particles, or waves,
depending. Even as testimonials
hardened into notebook fact.

Plausible rival hypotheses
will arise in court. The incident
began more suddenly than the victim
expected, and will last much longer.

Clone

Four should be enough of me for me. No, three.
They might not easily apprehend, but they can do,
and doing's the battle I get them to attend.

To send them out with grocery lists and day-to-days;
milk, bread, whatever I yen for between bread, they'll even
plate it carefully so I can keep on teasing out this stuff.

Parties, several at once, they drink like cops
filling late-month quotas, engage the feckless
literati with *The Phaedrus* while I seduce their wives.

That means course enrolment. Tuition. Tough;
I learn to play guitar unburdened during
their job interviews. Finally fangle origami.

It's a bit like being God, seeing myself from behind,
askance in the way you can't but want to. The sum
of our actions define me while they live my lives

as though committing crimes. Lately we don't look
each other in the eye. They're not reading dictionaries
in the off hours. Unfashionably late, on the skive

at the local, making fools of me. Unviable.
Soon and earlier than they think, with such retrograde
expectancy, they'll drown in the last air left them.

So it's a waiting game. Time for a fresh start; tonight
I'll hit the town and rake the coals they've left. I am
going to wear my favourite shirt, the brown one. Or am I.

Cyclops

There are envelopes with plastic windows,
they won't stop searching for you. Feeling owed,
when the last shopper's off the streets in bed,
your late carnations on the kitchen table fed
with 7-Up for perk, the kids asleep unwashed,
each blind eye will throw another unabashed
glance, and find nobody but the television left on
long after the collector had rung the bell and waited,
his watch face, and his own, unmoving, wan.
Not that there was much else he anticipated.

Dialectic Concerning the Deity's Benevolence

The bus is moving awfully slowly. Has it slowed down?
You know, of course, if it continues to move this slowly
we'll have to get off and take a cab. I feel that the bus driver
indicated through his body language that we'd arrive at
the route 12 connection, though he never did verbalize this.

Jonathan, you have to stop focusing on the bus,
it's something you can't control, and you're causing
yourself unnecessary stress because of it. Try to
think of something else.

I know, it's just very difficult to stop, when I can't tell
whether the bus driver understands that the bus needs
to be at the connection to bus 12 at 4:00 p.m.

Jonathan, please try to think of something else. The bus
and the bus driver are beyond your control. He needs to rest
at the main stops in order to keep to his schedule, so that
people who are expecting him at a specific time
don't miss the bus because he's gone too quickly.

I know, but it's very hard. It's difficult to stop. At least
my obsession will stop in, oh, six weeks or so. Maybe
he's prone to slowing down through this section of his route.
He may be inclined to do that.

Jonathan, please stop thinking about the bus.
Why not try to think about more constructive things,
or more pleasant things, like the sunshine?

Yes, the sunshine is all around me. The sunshine is blah.
Every time I look up, the sun is there. But this bus is still waiting
at a stop, and while the bus driver may be inclined to do that,
we will very likely miss our connection to bus 12,
unless we get off now and get a cab.

Jonathan, stop it right now. You have to stop
obsessing about these things beyond your control.

Yes, I know, but it's very difficult for me to stop
once I've begun thinking about how we need
to get to the connection for bus 12. I know
I'll stop when … perhaps the bus only appears to be
going more slowly than it once was, though in fact
it's travelling at exactly the speed it needs to be travelling.

Jonathan, the more you say it's difficult for you
to stop thinking about something, the more difficult
it becomes for you to stop thinking about it.

But we have to connect with the 12 at 4:00 p.m,
and it's 4:00 p.m. now, and he's been idling here
at a minor stop for an inordinate amount of time.
In all likelihood the bus driver has stopped here
at this minor stop rather than the main stop up ahead.
Perhaps he's stopped here to wait rather than the next stop.
You don't think he'll stop up ahead to wait again, do you?
We've been waiting at this stop for quite a long time now.
Excuse me. Excuse me, bus driver.

Jonathan! Stop that immediately. You are not going to start
questioning the bus driver about his decisions and the job
he's doing. It embarrasses me and insults him.

But I just want to discover why he's waiting
at this minor stop. For all of the waiting we've done
we could have been downtown by now, and we
wouldn't have missed our connection with bus 12.

He's doing everything he does for a reason, and it is not
necessarily all related to our needs specifically. Do you think
you know his job better than he does?

Well, I don't know ...

Have you ever driven a bus before?
Do you think you could do a better job?

I don't know. I mean, did you get a look at him?

First, myself. Then her, for it will always end with her, no matter how I may deviate in the telling. Where better to begin than the *ergo sum*, that essential component of so simple yet decisive a formula. For you see, in order to clarify the sordid, cloudy motives of my actions you must understand the me-ness of them. *Le moi.* The my. The mind. Did I say mind? I meant mine.

I could not have accomplished what I did had there been any considerate ratiocination of consequence on my part. Certainly there has since arisen, in late wakeful hours, the borborygmic stir of anxiety about the choices I've made, but let us not mistake these flatulent rumblings for a soul. In me, I fear, there is no moral centre, but processes, and the work of the natural chemicals on their thoughtless, secretive course through the bloodstream. So I will dispense with self-pity, and seek no sympathy either, but merely expect from you a dim comprehension of the indifferent facts to follow. How else can one acknowledge death except to prepare for it by translating the details?

And yes, my vanity will strive to appall the perverts with these proceeds, but as is often the case one succeeds only in titillating the puritans for the effort. We hadn't made love in months, she and I. Though that is neither

Several Takes

Being negatively capable,
     can I rightly consider myself
a perishable non-food item or novel
     element in this repetitive
environment? While exploring northern
     forests, or vacationing along
the Atlantic seaboard? Then, I am
     also a featherless biped, prone
to realizing I'll never play the Dane,
     nor ever again sing 'By the Rivers
of Babylon' in my boyhood kitchen. Also,
     when I say 'I', I could be referring
to someone else entirely, having mistaken
     him for me, as seen from a deceptive angle
or too great a distance. His past is
     a composite of anecdotes rigged
with discarded set dec. Crossing
     a room's threshold, he'll forget his purpose
and cling to an ideal version. He wears
     a louche smirk as if he's watching
a film in which he plays no role. You know,
     of course, when I say 'he' who I mean.
His shadow precedes him, describing
     the directions he may take in a voice
quieter than the wind not blowing
     and no one stepping across fresh snow.

Even

Stefan springs forth without remainder. After work
he hits the Classy Chassis. Everyone looks vaguely familiar.

And the food's better than, which is the enemy of antecedent
good. He slots a quarter and the automated fortune teller

relates intrinsic truths:
>   *Ha ha ha, it talks! Ha ha ha.* Drowning

the gallantry of well-spoken women who prognosticate
near the unplayable jukebox. Across the frozen pond

in Brown's yard the bronze-cast goat brandishes a bolt
for an asshole, licence plates dangle from the blow-torched tree.

Plus a moose silhouette. Each sculptural detail furnishes
a surreal idea of nature for this quarry town. Or for Brown.

From the tailings sluiced off the valuable leach,
from the wonderfully obvious main drag scene,

from frequent maladies, not Stef's, except for chronic gout,
from the unknown emergencies of his neglected teens,

he assembles his philosophy, his will. The notion actions
make a man doesn't apply, he's cancelled them out.

The remainder springs forth obliviously without Stefan.
Ha ha ha, it talks! Ha ha ha. Sure, it's not that funny, but still.

Odd

Then unbuoyant dread at the all-night
hot-dog stand. On the woozy cab ride home
the street turns trampoline, Olympic updates

play on ethnic radio. Cars lurch to the stops
like relics waiting for an archivist with foresight.
Sewer smells, primary, combine then cancel out.

Faces of the passersby broadly range
the zone of cranky and dissatisfied. What
happens badly comes in threes but never

does triangulate, while they waver, gather
patternless at crosswalks, not as sums
of chance but slim chances held against.

Probably, we're told, it's not success
or doing our job well that counts, but
to recuperate from unexpected failures.

The business district's scrapers look like saints
about to levitate, every ad's in love with us;
condo cranes are angels poised again to strike.

Fla.

Where want has ended
communities are gated, the sprawl

broken by box store malls, all of it
floating seven feet above sea level.

Spotless streets corsaged with palms,
the mostly vacant homes

house screened-in pools
off the back instead of yards.

Safe.
Not safe, but having purchased

a sense of security. We imagine
nothing but what surrounds us here.

Ensconced,
we steam in the hot tub

like sausages in our natural casings.

◇

A bald eagle steals an osprey's prey
mid-flight.

Snowy egrets dodge past barefoot
waiters toward the seltzered surf

like waiters without arms or trays.

The sun snaps one second into the next,
puzzle-piece perfect and clean

as our margarita ice.

A certain order finds its way.

If we see dolphins today
the fit will feel even closer.

◇

Jimmy Buffett calms the nerves
of the German woman buying

swim trunks for her nervous son.

Masticating is chewing. Expectorating
is spitting, and a crime. I don't know why

these mannerisms come to mind

while nature extends such courtesies
to us in its decline.

The outlet is a well-turned-out buffet.

Nictitating also feels important
to the moment. The vast air-conditioned

aisles quietly filling with it.

◇

Among the manatees and alligators
tangling in the Everglades,

beyond the walls of the enclosure,

something terrible is happening,
the likes of which we'd rather not see.

Sounds we'd rather not hear.
The ranger reloads his camera,

unaccustomed to this dilemma.

◇

Nightly self-policed, each encoded house
a curfew of sleeping couples

transparent to one another
as they can let themselves be,

truthful as strangers asking for directions.

Loss, regret, distress, all the anonymous
murdered selves relax on their nocturnal faces.

Tomorrow's forecast, like every other,
is what they are going to expect.

◇

The humidity is primitive: a florid stink of
ripe vegetable and camouflaged lairs.

Memory is dampened to a whiff
then masked by chlorinated pools,
barbecues, bourbon,

the new time of children.

We remember nothing but
what surrounds us.

◇

On the white-sand beach,
stark cherubs and tanned bathers

step haltingly into the sea
as if afraid they're returning

somewhere happily forgotten.

I wish I could describe it to you
with the big, wholesome metaphor of music:

these healthy buoyant tourists,

how the decorated yuccas and pastel
condominiums simply drain away

when the ocean's brilliant flag
swells in the outcast eye.

P eople round here, they'd drink out of a sweaty clog. I'd have given this town a right good bottoming and slung me hook ages ago if I'd proper dosh. Chance would be a fine thing. I'm as fit as a butcher's dog, mind, it's no' that I scurry from work, but all I get round the place when I smack the stones complaining for an honest eight hours is *go polish your metal somewhere else, we all have it hard*. The lot of 'em act sharp enough to cut themselves while the most interesting thing about 'em is they've got feet at the end of their legs. Wish they'd shut their laughing gear and just get on wi' it.

So th' day it's back to the pub for a quick sip of mother's ruin, or maybe splash out a bit, throw a large Scottish wine down the neck and clear the brain area. It's always noses to nipples in here, even the nooner, which keeps Kenny the 'tender grinning all over his boat and me with no stool to choose but one beside the lass with a face like a slapped ass and a smile like poison coming to dinner. I know the next bird over, quite a fancy piece, though she's all fur coat and no knickers. They call my shout, and how can I refuse these pigeons aught? You never know what's for afters. There's only been a coupla skirts me whole life that've been worth the hangover, but friends, aye, friends you must gather close to your soul and wrap them tight with hoops of steel, as the dead bard says. Besides, I'm no round-shirker, even on the dole. It's no' some deep secret why, just a pa's lesson to his whinging son a good while gone that stuck. The gab lit up

Slide Show of Uig

Willy, or Wally, no deciphering the brogue, sang his late dad's
verse outside the pub at the ferry pier, a Gallic clip we didn't
glean the gist of but knew it proved the old man's worth;
more than the strips of peat he used to flense from these hills

for everyone, for warmth. The weather's weird; competing in
a single patch of sky I hadn't seen so many takes on grey.
Bees bumble in the columbine and big dopey flies, recently
alarmed, dash their hopes against the fisher's window (stickered

I'm a Real Scot, a Highlander) with the industry of the unemployed,
like the frugal time-lapse-stillness swallows frame the air with
at each treed hairpin on the switchback road around the bay.
Like the delay when a moment's handed to the past, lending

improved vision, relief, but only for the back-directed glance.
Though this stop-motion sense might be the denatured stench
of naphtha and scorched metal that lances the brain from coal fumes
fuming out the cottage chimneys in this season's featured damp.

Big Pig, our neighbour, outdated for the table, seems unaffected
as she nozzles sprouting garnishes the sheep pass up. This avails
in no way the photogenic farm on which she lives or its
environs. Our side of the camera I can't recall with detail.

BBC World News

The country's dividing, towns burn for the old views
The courts are assuaging, more converts for church pews
Accusations flying, stones lathed for *Anons*
Armed children huddling, fresh fodder for cannons
The pipelines are leaking and central to public concern

The ships are embargoed, meds banned for the stricken
The rats have all jumped, now there's rest for the wicked
The coital ooh-aahing, crude pleas for forgiveness
Oppositions have risen, black sacks hood each witness
The cameras are rolling and soldiers have volumes to learn

Plastic tarp in the hole that remains of his house, a father's bridled fear
Sounds through the tent flap like laughter and football chants, fireworks,
 holiday cheer

Late second half Aston Villa was surging then blew a spectacular lead
After the break Simon Auld to discuss market flux and recovery speed

Insomnia

The flag and flab of an old man
gradually thinned by poverty.
The leftover thought. Groping,
but not quite copping a feel.
Slack-jawed, with your ear pressed
deep into the mattress, the springs
ping their torpedoed sound of drowned
metal, a chain-link turnbuckle long tossed
by teenagers off the river overpass,
worn by underwater current, turning out
rust for this new element. No, no,
it's your heart thumping the bed. Sleepless,
sleepless. How to keep oneself from harm,
invite tragedy into others' lives. Relish malice.
Never again to hear *Get in the fucking car.*
Waiting for that Charger with a full tank.
Where were you? Oh yes, the water
is lapping the road, even this late from thaw.
What water? Wakefulness rises
to the nostrils, threatens you with dawn.

Song for the Call of the Richardson's Ground Squirrel Whose Call is a Song for the Cry of the Short-Eared Owlet

In the cow pasture across the road, they may simply be
an eyelash trapping the dusk. They seem there, and there,
and there and gone. Prairie mirages. But the call is
unmistakable – syncope of blue sky, fear and the Swainson's
hawk's lethal dive. Jazz interruptions in a calm Saskatchewan evening.
Nothing anyone can say is more humourless. Imagine
three cats in a bag. Whoopee cushions. Jackknives
puncturing the tires on the bastard neighbour's
unmufflered Datsun. It's alarming enough
to make you want to run home and count the kids.
Who knows? With such fleet thieves' hands
perhaps they're lamenting their lack of pockets
before ducking back into invisible kingdoms;
what choruses and sudden confusions, casualties,
among the families in those dark territories.
When you live for so long beneath the horizon
there must only be a language of weeping.
Listen as they peer partially, cautiously,
back into the sunset world.

Repeat Offender

The cat has it right, plays dead
on the coolest plot of hardwood
as I wade from room to room

through a humid undifferentiated
pool of myself. With clammy hands
and a recidivist's empty resolution

I attack the dishes in the sink,
aftermath of a Dutch Master's still-life,
scrub the bathroom porcelain until

a nullity of contrast is achieved.
A field washed out by blizzard
or a snowy television's the cognitive

effect I'm after; cutting the switches,
pulling plugs on appliances might rid me
of the suspicion there's a guest

about to arrive who will refuse to leave
and won't add value to the evening.
The walls continue to inhale

and exhale electricity. Any moment
my quantum counterpoint,
the q to my p, spiffy and eloquent,

bearing another formula for optimism,
could appear and cancel both of us
in one last whimper of heat. But then

nothing would verify the cleanliness
and newly refined balance of this space
quite so thoroughly as my absence.

The Text May

You turned forty all afternoon,
and at every hour's sink you scoured,
you raged. The thought was gruel; your mind implored
like a Cheshire, like a carved gun

completing its bore, faking a heist
of the years that remained. But the text may survive,
though you were chafed, profane; sot in the creased
suit, wise, you'd give.

Leslie Farquhar was born in 1983 at Advocate Trinity Hospital in Chicago, at that dewy dawn hour when widows with undisturbed wealth are disgorged from penthouse apartments to walk toy purebreds down pleasantly vacant boulevards while brokers slip soundlessly from the Murphys of their mistresses to head directly back to work in yesterday's shirt and tie. That is, she was born in a time and place that determined her to be one of those for whom opportunities would always exceed her abilities.

Tracey and Reynold Farquhar lived in the suburbs of Hickory Hills just south of the city. They raised their daughter with middle-class means and morals and expected, as parents of an uncommonly beautiful girl do, that she eventually flourish in a world which showers reward upon people endowed with natural symmetry. Voted neither prom queen nor valedictorian, Leslie did, however, bring the football captain to graduation.

Competent at everything, expert at nothing, Leslie decided to become a dancer, which landed her in New York at twenty, but without success. She then attempted writing with similar expectations and even greater failure. This was due, in part, to her assumption that fascinating and exotic experiences, like the men in her life, would simply be attracted to her. At twenty-five, with a trail of publishers' rejection letters and one brief, futile marriage behind her, Leslie began to feel she could no longer drift but must swim directly for decisive moments. It was about this time she adopted a tone in conversations that made the most straightforward comment sound wildly suggestive to professional men within earshot.

Let us, as our imagination allows, leap forward ten years to discover Leslie in the midst of a swarthy July downpour in Manhattan, on her way to the temporary employment office. Capable, now, of dealing with disappointment only slightly less ungraciously than in her youth. It is here

Possibly About Everything and Nothing

Slabs the size of cities calve
and drift from Greenland glaciers.
Sightseers raise their cameras in victory.

The sun pixellates on the choppy waters
in whose flash-bulb pops flash
triumphant phrases yet to be considered

while a fresh pandemic invests
deeply in loose-knits and articles
plush or humid, undiscovered

like the extra in that low-budget film
appearing in every scene as atmosphere
we don't acknowledge nor can describe.

It wasn't the hours of television but
books that ruined us –
all the criteria for our disagreements.

What a song of panic before sleep.
We listen to the ringing phone dissimulate,
lying to everyone that we're not home.

The Photo Double

On the gimballed replica of the tall ship
the director's face is swallowed by a megaphone.

The cameras, correctly aligned, produce a seamless
waterline between the shooting tank and the Pacific
ocean behind it. Cloudy skies are ideal for this illusion.

Study the dailies, learn his moves. I am the mirror left
after the actor has used the mirrors up. The wide lens.

The scene requires the release of several thousand gallons
of siphoned sea water. Decommissioned jet engines
fill the sails on action. It will run fifteen onscreen seconds.

There's a delicacy born of dangerous
moments the producers are desperate to capture.

View playback. The lead's on-deck comportment
is casual, loaded with unrelinquished energies
cocked in slumped shoulders. Languid as a gorilla.

Tenderness confines its gestures to near misses, the use
of violence must always appear a life-saving measure.

Last looks. Final touches. An air horn blows.
The extras are miming. When the rubber sabre
strikes my arm I'll react like it's cleaved to bone.

Which has less to do with feeling pain
than understanding timing. Apply glycerine tear.

In the background all the British sailors
are Americans, all the French are Mexicans.
Esta muy contento de estar aquí. Back to the dailies.

They're about to roll again. Pretend. Be unreal.
Be more real than I have ever imagined.

Now, when I'm alone I often act
as though someone else is watching.
Each take costs fifty grand.

When

From here the outdoors is a dream sequence.
Distorted as through stressed aquarium Perspex
rather than glass. When I was young I'd hang
my head upside down over the arm of the sofa
so the furniture gripped the ceiling's shag
and historical blood rushed to the inverted heads
in family portraits. I marvelled at the unlofty
spaciousness we'd have in which to live.
But doorways were difficult to negotiate,
would become litigious. A raven large as a lion
lands, its talons hectoring bare branches
with what must be a sound like kitchen clatter,
dropped plastic cutlery, were I close enough to
catch it. You know, was outside not inside. And
minuscule. This reminds me of another lovely tableau:
in windy signatures along that rural route, the final
scrawl of poplar shadows at dusk. Memory can be
sketchy; embellishing atmospheric detail is essential.
The task has always been to keep the brain alive in time.
A calcium-binding protein found in cnidaria might
prevent decline; consider cinematic explosions
of the enhanced cosmic variety for a visual analogy.
When you think I'm inattentive, or when I step
cartoonishly high across thresholds, it's because
I haven't fully recovered from childhood.
A Portuguese man-of-war is a conglomerate
of non-sentient jellies, not the discrete creature
it appears to be. As we appear to be, for the most part.
In person, though, I am inevitably myself,
and can thread moments together even when
they happen as if they haven't happened.

American Ekphrastic

Run Time 1:41:26:096

From the side of an airstrip, framed in the bay door of a small hangar, two men watch a twin-prop Lockheed Electra rise cumbersomely over larger hangars in the middle ground. It is night and the air is thick with laden mist. The men are ill-matched, relatively incongruous; one is dressed in a dark military or law-enforcement uniform, his officer's cap jauntily askew, and the other, marginally taller, in a pale grey trench coat and black-band fedora. The buzz from the propellers swells as the plane passes overhead and the men's faces tilt skyward following its progress. A single taillight on the plane diminishes to the flickering speck of a star, the fuselage obliterated by the dense murk. The officer directs a sly look to the man in the fedora, who smokes while staring after the departed plane. They stroll out onto the tarmac in slightly staggered positions and as the officer begins to speak, a dulcet string arrangement of 'La Marseillaise' simultaneously descants. His tone is informal and he smiles as he talks, raising his eyebrows frequently to indicate wry commiseration or a mutually shared sympathy. After a pause, the man in the fedora answers the question posed him and the tone of conversation acquires an even greater sense of ease. The men walk away, side by side now, surrounded only by a few landing lights spilling onto the slick runway, music still playing, further into the fog, into obscurity with no apparent or foreseeable destination.

A girl lies in bed in a fitful delirium, a single phrase repeatedly issuing from her thickly lipsticked mouth. Though clearly in late pubescence, she is dressed fetishistically young for her age and wears her hair in pigtails. She opens her eyes, continuing the refrain until she registers an elderly man and woman at the bedside. The woman is kneeling and clasps the girl's hand while the man hovers closely. To his right, a window the size of a half-opened Dutch door posits a pasture fence and fallow fields beyond. The woman rouses the girl further from her liminal state with kind words and pats on the hand, and with relief the girl recognizes them. The woman removes the washcloth from the girl's forehead. A voice outside the window signals the presence of another man, who leans abruptly, and dangerously far, through the aperture to address the old man within. The girl is shocked. He is mustachioed, wearing a black suit and black-brimmed hat. As the two men speak, the girl bolts up in bed to refute the soundness of their claims, but the woman eases her back down with gentle remonstrations. The plaintive notes of a flock of unseen stringed instruments rises. The woman retrieves an empty glass from the night table and, still holding the washcloth, exits. Three men with beaming grins immediately take her place at the bedside, firing a tender volley of questions at the girl. She reaches out to caress the face of the nearest man, the eyes of all five men upon her, then begins to frame her own hypotheses, until she gesticulates with a tiny fist and finally extends an accusatory index finger at the mustachioed man. The men chuckle in concert at her apparent confusion and she raises her hand to her temple in a gesture of self-doubt. The older woman re-enters the room and the three moon-faced fools back away. The girl pursues her explanation about which the others remain unconvinced. A dog leaps to the bed and climbs into the girl's arms as she sits upright to greet it. She looks, the dog clutched firmly, less dismayed, perhaps even happy now. The darkness envelops them to an impulsive crescendo of strings, a racket of horns and angry cymbals.

Two men, stripped to the waist and holding hands, descend the stone steps of an ancient temple. Their faces are garishly painted, one in red, the other green. A throng of men surrounds them but parts to allow a path as they approach. The air pulses with incandescent fog and smoke, whose light bounces off sheer red banners and illuminates the encircling tropical vegetation. A boat, with the two men now aboard, reverses from the foot of the temple steps and the throng silently observes their departure. The sound of rain is heard, infused with eerie sustained notes from a Moog. The green-faced man pilots the boat with a blank stare while a static-filled transmission crackles from the helm radio. The red-faced man, squatting on the bow, not unlike a quadruped on its rear haunches, inclines his face to the downpour. The green-faced man leans forward with a worried look and cuts the radio off mid-sentence. The boat performs a standing about-face and the apparition of an immense stone bust materializes in semi-transparency, accompanied by fresh gusts of glowing fog. The giant stone head, vaguely Buddhist in cast, is sectioned into four equal crosscuts, roughly compartmentalizing the forehead, the eyes (sculpturally, in the Grecian style), the nose and the mouth. As the boat begins its forward progress, the green-faced man's head appears beside the boat in the same scale as the statue. His head is also a gauzy pretence, and their phantom aspects partially overlap. Still, rain dominates. The green-faced man's head turns in the direction the stone head blindly gazes. As he does, the boat becomes enshrouded by fog. Only the beacon atop its canopy remains visible, until it, too, is extinguished. A superimposed chopper flies into his head. An explosion erupts in figment, within a veil of jungle. Another chopper cuts across the flames. A male voice thinly rattles off two words. The fire fades. The hollow voice restates. The green-faced man merges with the bust, dissolving to leave only the statue, now a solid form. Both it and the remaining fog are consumed by blackness. Unabated, the sound of deluge continues within this fresh void.

The door to apartment 9732 opens inward with a rush of escaping oxygen or the flush of a pneumatic compressor, revealing a man who hides half-protected behind the corner of the doorway. There are contusions on his face and he holds a gun close to his chest. He peers out, then leans back into the room and beckons an unseen woman by name; she appears in deep background but then halts as he raises his other injured and bandaged hand in warning. Smoke, which saturates the air and is lit with high contrast, lends an aromatic notion to the atmosphere. Moving into the corridor, the man reconnoitres the few metres between the door and an open elevator before signalling her toward it. Apart from two aquamarine source lights embedded in the Egyptian-style carved stone wall and the interior cabin lamps of the elevator, a harsh light invades the surroundings at peculiar or unlikely angles. As the woman strides quickly past him into the waiting elevator, she inadvertently kicks over a scintillated piece of origami on the marble tiled floor. When she does this a bell sounds, barely discernible, and the collection of ambient noises heretofore unidentifiable assembles into music. Peripherally, he catches sight of the small tinfoil object and bends to pick it up. She watches him from the elevator. He holds it aloft; it is a unicorn. He smiles in acknowledgement. Another unseen man's voice is heard, out of thin air, and the man nods his head in agreement with the words spoken as he crushes the unicorn in his fist. With a look of gratitude on his face the man turns to join the woman in the elevator, whose eyes attend him with their questioning gaze. The elevator closes before he can turn again to face us. Exeunt.

We Are a Healthy Culture

The need for blood donations rises
as holiday weekend approaches.
— *news tickertape, CityTV*

A dish. A real dish, a deep dish.
Even the gormless simps and intellectual gaps surround her
with husky voices that get them places. Damn the normal
and its constant surprises. There is that face again and you
just can't pin the name. People do run into one another.
Between my vodka sodas I'll eat the ice. Time
is faster than God. And more painful. I
would like to remain forgotten. Thanks.
Christ, that's what I need, long-suffering
athleticism and confidence to creep
in like a voice-over on the late show.
The one beside her with the bitten lip, hard as nails,
ordering another neat, she's looking this way.
Death is transparent. It gets in your underwear.
I'm B negative. Not a rare type.
Today wears fashionable clothing, trying hard
to innovate its minutes. Displays of disinterestedness,
shared lethargies – there are robots, literally,
on the television.

City Living

I am not who I think I am. The longitudes are off.
Despoiled, aging's aged me bare. Spotting
the ring she pulled the ripcord at her end
of the conversation and recoiled.

◇

The moment grew wide smugly. My glass drained
down to ice. His uncollected face hung near. There
is no memory here. It comes after, a slurry. The moment
grew wide with the one decision I could bear.

◇

Me top-notch slovenly, the dress her best,
and lovely, festooned with a shark's tooth of skin
at her breast, a sideways grin. Most often when I'm
thinking nothing I'm already thinking something else.

◇

This is a lark. You threw me a *don't fail now*
confidence. The nod was a pact. Which didn't
stop the pool cue's arc, these friable acts –
my teeth from caving, then the dark.

Streetcar Monologue

Charlie, ancient red
life bomb
          secondary systems

you put a knife to my throat
my throat area
I'll charge you with fucking murder

aim
then aim

enemies

I hate Harry Potter
and all men

Mostly Bags got a good score. – Yeah. Eric told me. What about her, though, who's she? – Some titless wonder he met at Happy Time. – Yeah, well, Mostly's a sucker. – But he's got the choice experimentals, you know? – I remember a time it'd hit you for nine hours. – Yeah, you'd take a quarter hit … – You'd walk into the blue church and be gone for three days. – I turned into a crow and flew away once. That doesn't happen anymore. – What the fuck are you talking about? – The good old days. – Did you see that? See that? Sometimes I just wanna take a stick and … Not good! – There she is. – Who? – Mostly Bags' lady business. – She is pretty hot. – He's kinda got all the markets cornered, doesn't he? – He's never come close to the blue church. – Doesn't need to. – What the fuck are you talking about? – I mean … – Do you have his number, or should we just go over? – Over where? We just wait here. – Fuck sakes, when'd he tell you that? – Just don't be yourself when he gets here. – Thanks. Very kind. – And don't mention Eric, they're not talking. – What's her name again? – I don't know, she's from the States. She just showed up. – It's too fucking hot out here. I haven't been

The Shape of a Casuist

I can't hold it any longer,
won't cling to the thought

that things themselves are not
what science can explain,

only their relationships.
Invariant design,

for example, of the American
Standard exposed me to unwanted

outward elements. To have to be
alone and desire it to be thus.

Nor is the Crane true-formed,
sculpted to the animism of that bird

even though its cold, smooth geometric
touch might soothe the unprotected.

But an Armitage, the exact contour
and depth of my face, by this strange

affinity eases the ambiguity I suffer.
Divine or comic. About Duchamps, say.

A paradise! Paradise awaits
as though in hectic fervour for me.

He called it ready-made. He named
it *Fountain*, something else entirely.

Tautology

On viewing the Guggenheim's Kandinsky show
from top to bottom, his last to earliest piece, beginning
at the end and so proceeding to the beginning again,
along the declination of that tornadic rotunda I met
a man halfway down, though he was halfway up,
who engaged me in a solipsistic conversation
about, well, himself, circular notions really,
at the alcove covering '22 to '33, calling for
a moral revolution in his own convictions, whose depth
and range I tried to match, but lacking true intensity
drew back, or up the incline, as it were, spiralling
forward this time through the painter's own transitions,
left the waffler steps behind in his state of recondition,
until, resolve in tailspin, stress levels spondeed, that is,
teeth set, trap shut, clapped tight, eyes wide, I spun,
trochoidal, and nodded assent, more a ploy to exit
past than listen, but the more that I agreed with him
the more he dug in his heels to argue contra my position.

This Object Has Been Assigned Aesthetic Value

The compartments are not holes, vessels,
hollows, voids; are not nothing.
The compartments bear the interests of
the negatively defined and amoral.
The compartments are representational
on both figurative and literal levels.
The compartments are of the variety
that rarely allow for topical references.
The compartments actively reconstrue
any moment's low-yielding torpor.
The compartments have proportions
that admit one human being at a time.
Whose body acts as a natural baffle
to the otherwise elegant acoustic within.
The compartments when unoccupied
resemble a roomful of well-lit Rothkos.
The compartments are scientifically
principled and incline toward symmetry.
The compartments seem to approach
'I love you' with an honest misgiving.
The compartments often don't exceed
28 KB of information or virtual space.
The compartments harbour memories,
which snicker like jovial assassins.
The compartments are categorical,
but not in any swiftly understood sense.
That no one listens is significant,
though they emit no audible frequency.

The compartments confirm cognitive
habituation orients the viewer's taste.

In the broken yolk of dusk, indistinct birds diminish in number and furtive volume, remembering previous dawns, a greater happiness. The sky is a vast dam of light patched with clouds of straw and mud; he pays no homage, the weight of his own nature so heavy upon him as to prohibit reflection. Death is coming for him, but something worse has already transpired. Rallying to a forsaken, penultimate effort, jerky footsteps carry him back through the door. His shambling prospect collapses on the bed. Each movement, primitive now, furls inside him to disappear as involuntary impulse. The bed, still made but creased, lit lamp, bathroom kit, her overnight satchel, even she, do not stir but declare their attendance to one another, having relieved themselves of his perspective, looming though it once was. If one or two minutes had been exchanged this would have ended differently.

As if genuflecting toward prayer, some derelict ancient ritual, he rises with her near-conscious body and she swallows furious moans until her arms begin to talon and shield. Blood springs from his boots and off his hands as he retrieves the knife again and again from her chest, desperate to bestow life. Out of an unwinding embrace he withdraws across the room, conceals the weapon along this panicky recoil. What she assumed

Vertebrate

Something ungulate was slain somehow, stumbled
in the tangled brome and popped a knee, tried climbing
higher ground to lick an entry wound too late,

run down by early hominids who'd come trampling through
the kill site, threatened, ill-fed. Or, untagged, unowned,
picked off by joyless locals from the road and left for dead.

Carcass gone, a pulse of nutrient for the soil, lying long
enough for bones to string a necklace in the overgrowth,
their own cairn, until we humped up the unfarmed ridge

and they detonated underfoot. What with my spurned
hips and joints, there's no justifying stooping low,
near to fours, to investigate and learn, unclasp one pearl:

size a fist, heft a hand grenade. Now it haunches,
specimen on the desk, like a plaster counterfeit beside
the Zippo, a few ballpoints, and doesn't do a thing

while I adjust the lumbar cant of my office chair.
There. That's fine, as far as I'm concerned.

Several Occasions for Happiness

I've grown obsessed with preservation,
fold bedsheets crisply as unread books, stop clocks,
search for signs of eternity when buying produce.
If I shift my gaze to familiar faces and objects
with simplicity and without aspiration, I can stare for
hours and none of them will change. That which moves
away from me isn't necessarily afraid and that which
moves toward me is not always in love, I've learned
to say with cautious honesty, surrounded as we are
by the cavalcade of powers and lights and agencies,
some of which I'm for but also some
I am against – a happy coincidence I can be
both at once. Of happiness, I forget what I have done
so imagine several occasions for it. They have many
likenesses, are each alike in part or whole, like most
of what's beyond my grasp. They're nameless as seconds.
They envelop, in their inane, fog-like disregard for details,
the bulk of what's transpired. Once I could conjure,

They take it without prejudice. They alter
something crucial in me as easily as conjugating
verb tenses. They confiscate my recklessness,
replacing it with refinement of taste. They take
their time. But they mustn't take my island.
It's all I have left to remind myself. The weather
here today is exactly as I remember it yesterday,
as mild as the week before. I'm convinced
this is remarkable, that this slight breeze is here
while the island remains, is theirs, too, but wondrous,
because it is. It is a perfect day for a swim.

The Clones' Brief Tenure

i. The First Reads *The Phaedrus*, Abridged

Now within the heavens are many
spectacles of bliss upon the highways.

Down here I'll call the wind avenues of wrecked music,
and that anemic verge of yews lamping wiry shade
along the urban growth boundary its feeble instrument.
So, too, the ring of each coin's cheap alloy
is a congratulatory note to this tinny autumn air

for such a succinct voice, with no appreciable distance
between the sound made and the sound heard as the coins
escape the hole over-laundering's worried through my pocket.
A horse from the roadside pasture crashes the fence, humours
metonymy then clamours with impatient hooves into day-end

gridlock. All this moving about breeds souls, I've read.
That's me, immortal matter, a smattering of universe made
coherent by reason. I'd love to kettle up late thermals,
view those aforesaid roadside exhibitions, but my wings,
already wasted and destroyed (same book), prohibit.

This means, then, that this means nothing, goddamnit,
right down to the threadbare rift in my trousers
which admits only vast indifference to my attention,
to its supposititious self, and to the nothing it also is
amid the rest that is also not within reach.

But such as have taken the first steps to the celestial
highway shall no more return to the dark paths.

ii. The Second Surfs the Net

Cleveland is lonelier and angrier without King James.

Lady Gaga, while wearing guts for garters, has begun
to weep openly during her concerts.

Patrice Brisebois visited the children's burn ward
and the phones rang off their hooks.

After three Red Bulls in the helicopter, Jessica puked
during her morale-boosting visit to Afghanistan.

Gwyneth and Britney both wowed with risqué gowns.

Oprah says the great thing about life is
it's the one thing we all have in common.

GSP continues to perform feats of diverted
sexual energy, and will finally fight in Toronto.

When Lindsay's drunk she feels better looking,
that she's better at most everything.

Dean Young leased a young heart on the open market.

CERN researchers are close to witnessing a Higgs boson,
which they affectionately call the God particle.

Merriam-Webster has announced 'austerity'
is the word of the year. The runner up is 'pragmatic.'

Snooki's having trouble finding shoes to match the bag,
and tweeted *it's all just a big ball of fuckness.*

Jackie's own teammates tried to injure him at practice.

The day Captain America was killed by an assassin's bullet
Jean Baudrillard also died, of a pointless illness.

Allan Baumgartner, funeral director and Texan,
auctioned off Lee Harvey Oswald's coffin for 87 big ones.

Miley whiffed a bong of salvia, laughed uncontrollably
then had a vision of her absent fella.

Who is the future Mrs. Tony Romo? I can tell you.

iii. The Third Reads the First

When I read *anaemic verge of yews lamping wiry shade*
along the urban growth boundary I read
stand of trees casting shadows on the edge of town

and think I have reduced his thoughts, insulted him,
or oversimplified the yews, but no,
        they have only grown

more complex since he laid eyes on them,
if he saw them at all and they weren't fabricated
        for the line to convey meaning of
                        another order entirely,

and now I'm stalled on the words, trying to uncover
a clue to the yews' reality, a stark hint of certitude,
        but find myself thinking instead about
the rapidity of urban expansion,

and inevitability – the likelihood
those yews, close as they were to the city limit,
have by now been expeditiously hewn to create more
        living room, if they ever did exist.

And about death. The tone is rife.
But it's not from death or ambiguity
        that I want protection; those trees are close

to what memories are like,
which I am often in the business of retrieving,
elusive and puzzling as troglodytes as they can be,
        though I'm still hung up on that horse;

the closest I can come is how I occupy
a sudden recess of thought, become unreal,
        possibly only time and energy
borrowed from some larger entropy,

        easily misplaced in the non-second
my mind takes to cajole persistence back – unlike
those drivers stopped in traffic

who have already propelled themselves
forward out from the cars,
past the dinner table, perhaps undressed

without a word to loved ones, and climbed
aboard their raft of sleep – here
        I am. I am right here;

whether or not those yews will survive,
    when the troglodytes appear, and from where
the horse, will be my safeguards.

About the rest I'm unsure, it may be
    he's missed the mark, misinterpreted,
so I'll go check the source.

Ten Views from an Unreal Dwelling

[In the southwestern Ontario town, a forty-foot, white-painted tower stands beside the newer transit station, which whisks commuters to their metropolitan destinations eight times daily. Chipped and rusted from weather and disuse, off limits, the perched holding tank has a chute jutting over the tracks, having long ago poured tonnes of processed flour into patient railcars. Here and there in the evening-kissed backyards, children wearing cherry-blossom, verdigris, aubergine or crimson-coloured jerseys practice footwork and dekes before legging it to their soccer matches on the manicured pitches of the high school grounds. Beer bugs and fresh brick dust fleck the air with deflected sunlight, also gleaming from the waxen blades of sticky ryegrass and Kentucky blue. Fences between the close-set homes block the wind so that the cedar shrubs remain sufficiently undisturbed for spiders to take up residence, too. The next development over, cranes and shovellers sleep in long-necked bird poses near the exposed foundations of unfinished houses. Gravel piles lean against the sky, tall as the basements are deep. A wide suburban street lined with sapling maples runs through the finished neighbourhood. It is empty of cars, but for the packed double driveways nuzzling each set of garage doors, which offer a satisfying geometric repetition into the vanishing point. Across Thompson Creek, culverted under the asphalt, the road ends at tumbledown barbed wire that fences off cornfields, where a heron was once seen plummeting dead into the winter stubble. Although you can't take in the sea here, far as it is away from this place, its presence is felt in a certain briny ozone tang. If you wait past twilight, a train whistle blows through.]

Untimely Death in the Food Court

He ass-over-teakettled down a dozen stairs,
    flailing like a mechanism gone wrong,
a cartoon clock whose hands pay out
    time at delirious speeds, then stop.
To finally be the cynosure at this foolish
    juncture, splayed on the beige tiles
under a halo of his kids' shakes and fries.
    That day he described the farm to them,
where their kitten was romping unscathed
    and no car sped toward her crossing.
It may have been the overloaded tray,
    it may have been his foot found only space,
obstructed by the shopping bags. The look
    in his eyes a widening disbelief
at his own demise. Obviously, was the final
    thought that fell between his misstep
and surprise, there is a theme at stake
    here, its variations endless. Not love
but to have at least escaped cruelty and
    politics, appreciated my brief legacy,
none of which saved each day from its defeat.
    Or, with all this talk about not knowing
what can we? Or, I never could stomach
    the sound of summer rain that sizzles
on pavement like all this frying meat.

Three gins past midnight, Richard McNally sat hunched over the bar at Sun Valley Parlour, considering his penchant for bad locales. The slouch was a habit picked up years ago after Gas Munce broke parole and decided to check his pulse with a sap. The gin was an older story. He was about to call Gladys for a fourth when cherries began to wink through the rain-bleary windows. Two reds skidded into the Casa Mendoza lot across the street. Automatically he stubbed his butt and made to get up, then eased back down on the stool. It wasn't his business anymore. Besides, it was soaking outside and the civvies hadn't even arrived.

'Gladys, blow me one more of your liquid kisses.'

The Mendoza, one of Aldridge Pick's places, squatted on a strip of mean dime-novel bars, addict flops and dingy bungalow motels. A place whose neon forever flashed *Vacancy*, but hour by hour managed a healthy head of cabbage. Ray 'Boy' Robertson, a homicide badge, saw McNally coming and stopped him at the door to room 12.

'Dickie the Dick. Hell.' Ray, decked out in a compelling argument against fashion, complete with clashing tie, stood close enough to him to swing something heavy and connect.

'You smell like my third wife. On the hire, or chasing sirens and whores now?' he asked, slicking the drizzle through his thinning blond hair.

'Just ruining my life at the Parlour, looking for second chances,' McNally said, sparking a damp cigarette. 'Got one?'

'No boss in it for you, but go ahead. A dirty mash job.'

Like most corpses, hers wasn't keen to offer up any secrets. She'd been tussled all right, so firmly no words could cling to her pulped features long enough to settle on a description. But the scene was too tidy for a

A Certainty Recurs for Gabe Foreman

Eyeing those I should be with like marks
I smoke a cigarette instead, apart, and listen
to them grieve their grievances as I would

had I any. Like skipping vinyl I might have talked
germanely about how easily issues complicate,
but this would stall conclusions. I might

have argued the matter. Here my obligation
to silence assumes an easier posture.
Thought-balloons – *I don't want to die*

remarkably but as a bankrupt social virtue does;
the hoarder's fascination with belongings exceeds
the watcher's fascination with the hoarder;

don't let me end up as a photo beside someone
I've been only kind to – balloon then pop.
Can I say I know myself? Confidently, neither

before nor since. The group moves in ahead,
collectively connipted, griping toward the door,
their bodies to their lives as water is to waves.

Symptom Diary

Even antimatter is in decline
    as things heat up before the big
        cool-down. In the time it takes

a fox or wolf to form in the womb,
    the billion atoms of my body will
        have fled to more energetic fields.

I wave goodbye but as they leave
    duplicates arrive and occupy
        their place, determined as the kits and

pups. The past piles up inside this me,
    and a foraging unromantic melancholy.
        We remember our own lives

only slightly better than novels
    we've read. When I consider this
        debris I'm reminded of an image

broadcast yesterday. From a war
    about to be fought, or ongoing
        and unwinnable, without soldiers.

With Love, Jan

but to go there
the mind
endlessly
is singing
    – Sappho

    The poems we haven't read
    must be her fiercest:
    imperfect, extreme.
        – Jane Hirschfield

[These are not propositions, but several halves of several potential metaphors.]

Like wind turns a strand of exhaled smoke
in a helical twist like a skipping rope, before it vanishes.

[A dialogue, in its call and response, would enact this explicitly.]

[Humpback whales suspend themselves upside down and perpendicular to the direction of sea currents before they begin to sing.]

[Being personal and being intimate are significantly different qualities. Being personal risks the writer's self-awareness, being intimate risks the reader's sense of self in relation to another.]

[If one considers our associative intuition of metaphors as a pre-linguistic event of consciousness, one might be tempted to understand language use as half-formed metaphors exchanged at the goodwill instant of their gesturing across.]

[The is of a metaphor is an apology to silence.]

Like the hind-shot wolf who wobbles,
like an unfletched dart, toward his target, the treeline.

[At the moment we recognize someone is crying out of joy and not sadness, the heart tacks.]

[During engaging discussions people will gesture with their hands, arms, faces, in manners as unpredictable as the effect a brisk wind will have on the flight path of a butterfly. Or in the way a sudden light source inflects the vector of a moth.]

[So meaning doesn't exist, as such, but rather occurs.]

[When someone we know well is alone we cannot know who they are. They become unfinished metaphors (brought into relation with, compared and contrasted to *what?*), whose meaning for us dwells in a deferred state, as though adrift in another element.]

Like the caffeinated earworm that repeats,
like a hound circling to find its spot to sleep.

[A single honeybee will return to its hive and transmit the location of the more rewarding foraging sites to thousands of other bees by way of a 'tremble,' or 'waggle,' dance. The dance consists of runs and circular or zigzag bodily movements; the direction of the runs indicates the relative position of the sun to the foraging site, and the waggle's duration is correlated to the distance between the site and the hive.]

[It is said that up to 80 percent of meaning conveyed in a dialogue is derived from facial expressions, posture and other physical gestures.]

Like people who appear not to need people
come to need people who appear.

[The more intimately we know a person, the fuller their silent gestures become for our understanding of what they attempt to mean.]

[What do we mean when we speak of gestures? What does *gesture* mean?]

[possibly
the delicacy of her wrists, moving
as she spoke, unnerved me.]

[The writer's attitude *anything goes* does not go far. It is a monologic misunderstanding of language, to believe that using language necessarily entails a relativistic insensibility rather than a resonant undecidability that seeks to inform all aspects of apparently exclusive or contradictory contexts.]

Like bees hovering, static in the solar glare,
like keloids on their skin of air.

[It is to write with the presumption that one can never, and therefore should never seek to, acquire wisdom through communication.]

[Which is not to say that there are no meaningless things, and that they cannot be beautiful. Quite the contrary – take dancing, for example.]

[Like a metaphor, a gesture entertains the likelihood that it both is (moves toward being) and is not (remains unfulfilled in its desire to be) the objects of its attention.]

[In much the same way physicists resort to spatial metaphors to describe time and temporal metaphors to describe space, philosophers and poets alike rely on non-metaphorical language to explain the concept of metaphor.]

[However unintentional, conversational gestures are the body's inescapable brashness; its truth.]

[The human brain is like a Hadron Collider in miniature – language is sets of discrete photons, the collisions are metaphors, and the debris, splintering off as indiscrete waves and particles in incalculable directions, is meaning.]

Like the god of the sea who beckons us in,
like those at their windows landlocked by the interim of hills.

[The more complex the system of mechanical parts the greater chance there is for a malfunction of the system. The more complex the system of conceptual parts the greater the chance for discovery within the system.]

[Lonesomeness, loneliness, aloneness: the distinctions and similarities between them.]

[Incidents of fatal grey whale strandings proliferate due to mid-frequency sonar pulses sent out in increasing numbers from U.S. military submarines conducting drills in the Pacific. The latest mandate calls to further extend the coastal range of these drills.]

[Silence, someone wrote, throngs.]

[You cannot sustain an intimate discussion in absentia, be it a temporal or spatial separation, as much as you may attempt to continually clarify your intention across the divide.]

Like the six-frame drift of sound from an image that repudiates
wilful disbelief. Like value unsynced from the going rates.

[Our memory resists this impasse in its reimagined recollections, as does writing, which, in its way, is a species of memory; the mind's ability to pause mid-current, cant across flow and sing to itself in another key.]

[Time flows over us. We pass through time. These are not simply symbolic statements, though they are of a metaphoric order.]

Like the cabbie who takes a wrong turn innocently,
his hands constant on the wheel. Like a miller against his grain.

[Worker bees are inexplicably disappearing. Their colonies are collapsing as a result. It's been diagnosed as a syndrome arising from the combination of extenuating ecological factors rather than as a singular pathogenic effect.]

[Being alone in a room together. Just that. There is wonder in mere presence.]

[To describe an intimacy is personal, to undertake to gesture is intimate.]

Like the blossom of her youth so, too,
will my pain fade. Like memory's chagrin at being left behind.

[Her jeans were covered in honey when she arrived at my apartment that day. The jar she bought at the farmer's market had broken over her lap in the car. The look on her face, the swarm of her hands as she explained herself, were eloquent and impressive as _____]

[A well-wrought metaphor that renews its tense each reading.]

[The sun, sifting through the gang of things seen; oceans of it for all of us.]

I am afraid of articulate light, and the wind, and hands and
flowers that are necromantic in some countries. And the frown
of memory passing like wind sweeping the boughs, like wind
I am afraid of my soul. I am afraid for my soul caught
in the trees as the wind rises. Like the bleating noises
below the trees. Well after the moment an animal refuses
to struggle. It's difficult to believe I am not eternal.

God, you look good. No, I haven't grown.

Whip Pan

There's movement overhead. My eyes, moving
    faster than colour, draw a bead. Of this, I'm not
in control. I hasten home to the online bird identifier
    before the outstanding features are buried under
heaps of perceptual trash that inveigle
    past my filters. Hours later, the computer is
glutted with my undivided attention.
    I become about as real as a book's intended
audience. An irksome disappointment
    focused on nothing in particular begins to stir,
is recognized, inexpertly soothed by self-forgiveness,
    then closes its eyes. This happens more quickly than
my retinas' flicker across the screen's fixed points.
    The intervals between sleep grow longer.

She is in a place, she thinks. Where? An inappropriate term. Other questions fail her. She feels like she's ... no, wrong again, she begins once more. Elemental whiteness. Theoretical whiteness, utter absence of darkness in which contrast has been abandoned; she does not know that she can see. Confined to a space in which she cannot stretch or turn, though she is not uncomfortable. Nil by none. She is limbless, no remainder, but gropes beyond herself in blind phantom extension. Pellucid. She is unbound by an extraordinary deliverance from feeling. She is standing, she lies prone, she breathes, she is drowning, she rushes toward, she waits until, she is dressed for a date, she has no skin or bone, she is floating, she is rooted, buried, she thinks of herself, she is no longer of, iconic, but as if, unbonding the way electrons slip from an unstable atom – if nothing can be said to explode against a singular expanse of emptiness discernibly. An idea. Nil by naught.

How long? Duration is immeasurably slow or instantaneous. Had she been flailing at something before this became and movement ceased, or movement grew imperceptibly rapid, unrecordable? She is certain there was prior experience by which she defined quantities, but the belief is disappointing. Reference has evaporated. She is unsure of was and will be. She is not here, she convinces herself she is thinking this right now. She is not here. Infinite sphere, centre everywhere without circumference.

Corpsing This Century

I know what you are about to say and you know what
I'm about to say. This turns our conversation into a gas.

Despite pre-emptive vocal exercises I still avoid your eyes,
stare at the space due left of your head and pretend I've just

come to, try to forget what you've said and will repeat;
but anticipation throws my better, composed self into a shit-

eating grin. When you use words like that I can't help it,
the fascination's morbid with me – *history*, *politics* eject

like plastic furniture from their seamless moulds, accumulate
unpatented, synonymous with landfill. Our miscues are

grave and the retakes no picnic. Because we're never not
aware of our surroundings. If you and I were in a Herzog

these would be the lines we couldn't get past, landing on the gag
reel as a gaff, though they're the lines we'd continue to recite

until we nailed the scene. But we're not. In a film. So
these replays keep playing on a loop. Similarly, art resulting

from the exhaustion of easy living provokes a stifled laugh.
I should say absurdity sets in earlier and earlier. Whose was

that exhibit, the sculptural gack suspended in the dark only after
the opening ended, the patrons left? There's a memory, too,

that makes me crack; a friend falling in slow motion from another
friend's horse. I've reduced it, for deft recall during crises,

to his look of surprise and the expression of air leaving him
on impact. The serious is so ripe, a cathedral for hysterics, really.

When I convinced myself the man slumped against me in emerg
last night was only sleeping, scanned the room for loved ones

to come nudge him awake, nothing seemed remotely funny. Even
allowing the silence and proximity. What happened next, as you've

guessed, was approximately the same as what didn't. Composure's
about timing. You mustn't equate deadpan with a winning performance.

Super Slo-Mo

At the speed of, say, a dark interior
   Benjamin Moore, Rafa executes a serve
unfair in its perfection. Noble and cruel.
   The standing O's a given but the moment's
been divided into hi-def frames of motion so
   the details float above the lawn at Wimbledon.
As the second dilates a million years there's
   no need to fix my gaze, the eye roams
unherded, articulate in this telescopic scale.
   It's like spying continental drift or the onset of rust,
radar-gunning the velocity of sloths, the phosphorus cycle
   run to completion. It spans the cradle to the grave
for giant clams. Now I fathom the rate manganese
   nodes wrap themselves in more of themselves
twenty thousand leagues below. As gradually
   as boulders coughed up by the sea are worn
smooth as saddles and anvils, the Schwartzer Adler
   in Leonberg thaws into a poignant symphony
for one boy, lonely Schelling, on his way from Latin
   school. Earlier, through suspended grains of sand
he watched, distracted from his lesson, water drops
   tick tick tick from icicles and ricochet off the sill
like confetti made of glass. Once, long ago,
   I climbed a tree, a sycamore, in which I felt
content. I remember thinking then not that time
   was eternal, just not about time at all.

Zero Kelvin

Gentle patriots of the suburbs whose faith
is an acronym for fibre access in the home,
where none means no one thing and news
the plural of new; all is flux, nothing abides.

Yet you reside, so rise from dinner parties, pause
your footie PVRS – *it doesn't rain like this in Astrakhan,
does it, Andrej? Zilch, Kelvin. Absolutely nada* – and
gather in the barren bulbs of muffled cul-de-sacs to scan

the subdivided sky, modulated by the bit-stream flow
and low electric yield. The constellation of your faces
forms a dazzling array. Each swivels toward spare
signals as they travel on their cold way out. Unimpeded

as your unlit sons and daughters bedding down in
parks and foreclosed fields, ruining their pretty hair.

Notes

Epigraphs to the poems are from 'In Your Big Dream' (in *31 Letters and 13 Dreams*, Richard Hugo, 1977), 'Feast of the Ascension, 2004. Planting Hibiscus' (in *Green Squall*, Jay Hopler, 2006), 'You in Sardis' (in *The Complete Poems of Sappho*, translated by Willis Barnstone, 2009) and 'The Lost Love Poems of Sappho' (in *Come, Thief*, Jane Hirshfield, 2012).

The unusual dialect in 'Cory on the Bash Awhile' is the result of an admixture of lines of dialogue lifted from the television show *Coronation Street*, lines of conversation overheard in numerous Scottish pubs and lines of my own contrivance.

'The Text May' is a homonymic translation of David O'Meara's poem 'The Next Day,' with the first line intact.

The first and last couplets in the first section of 'The Clones' Brief Tenure' are taken from Plato's *The Phaedrus*. Translated by R. Hackforth, 1952.

Information about bees and their dance routines in the poem 'With Love, Jan' has been paraphrased from 'The flight paths of honeybees recruited by the waggle dance,' in *Nature* (J. R. Riley, U. Greggers, A. D. Smith, D. R. Reynolds, R. Menzel, May 2005).

'Super Slo-Mo' is for Alayna Munce.

Acknowledgements

Earlier versions of some poems have appeared in *Arc, Event, The Fiddlehead, The Malahat Review* and *Riddle Fence*. The author also gratefully acknowledges the support of the Canada Council for the Arts, the Ontario Arts Council and the Toronto Arts Council.

With gratitude to Christopher and Lindy, Steve and Janet, Matt and Charmaine, Zameret Kleiman, Mary Dalton, Don McKay, Shane Rhodes, Elyse Friedman, and to director Jeremy Munce and the cast of Eyewitness Testimony.

 With love to my parents, Ron and Garie, and to my family, Jeff and Tracy, Rhea and Kirk, and my beautiful niece, Sophie. You are an ever-present source of strength.

 Many thanks to Alana Wilcox, Leigh Nash and Evan Munday at Coach House, for their expertise and kindnesses.

 To Michael Helm for weighing in on the Page One project.

 To Karen Solie and Kevin Connolly for being the first readers for many of these poems. Kevin's encouragement was the prime motivation for this book. And to my editor, Jeramy Dodds, who rode the manuscript through its paces, and who reconfigured the boundaries of my imagination in the process.

About the Author

David Seymour's *Inter Alia* was nominated for the Gerald Lampert Memorial Award. He lives in Toronto, where he works in the film industry.

Typeset in Aragon and Aragon Sans, from Canada Type.

Printed at the old Coach House on bpNichol Lane in Toronto, Ontario, on Zephyr Antique Laid paper, which was manufactured, acid-free, in Saint-Jérôme, Quebec, from second-growth forests. This book was printed with vegetable-based ink on a 1965 Heidelberg KORD offset litho press. Its pages were folded on a Baumfolder, gathered by hand, bound on a Sulby Auto-Minabinda and trimmed on a Polar single-knife cutter.

Edited by Jeramy Dodds
Designed by Alana Wilcox
Author photo by Jordan Samuel
Cover photograph of Kate and Pippa Boothman by Nicholas Boothman

Coach House Books
80 bpNichol Lane
Toronto ON M5S 3J4
Canada

416 979 2217
800 367 6360

mail@chbooks.com
www.chbooks.com